Dad, **Where Are YOU?**

"I just want my daddy"

Dr. Ken Fuller

Jeremiah 29:11

11 For I know the thoughts that I think toward you, saith the Lord, thoughts of peace, and not of evil, to give you an expected end.

Table of Contents

Book Dedication 1

Introduction 2

About the Author 3-4

Chapter 1: The Missing Piece 5

Chapter 2: The Day My Father Returned 12

Chapter 3: The Vanishing Hero 19

Chapter 4: The Void of a Father's Presence 26

Chapter 5: Finding Myself 32

Chapter 6: The Fragile Bonds of Fatherhood 40

Chapter 7: The Unseen Struggle: A Father's Journey Through Love, Guilt, and Redemption 49

Chapter 8: Fatherhood: A Journey of Imperfection and Grace 57

Book dedication

This book, *Dad, Where Are You?*, is dedicated to my children—Niaysha, Kamdyn, Kamaria, Keniah, and Kenise. As a young father, I often struggled to reconcile my inexperience with the responsibilities of parenthood, and at times, I fell short of meeting your needs. This story is my way of sharing the challenges I faced in fatherhood, and the struggles I had with my own father, in the hope that it will shed light on the difficulties many fathers face while raising their children.

This book is also a testament to the deep love I have for you, despite any shortcomings. My desire has always been to love you as a father should.

I dedicate this work to all fathers who, like me, have struggled to voice their challenges. You don't have to bury the pain or shame—whether it's because the father wasn't there, or due to your own struggles with being the father you want to be. I believe in your ability to be the father you aspire to become. My hope is that this story offers guidance, strength, and the courage to face fatherhood with clarity, and ultimately, helps us answer the question, *Dad, where are you?*

introduction

Dad, Where Are You? is a heartfelt exploration of fatherhood, reflecting on the challenges, struggles, and growth a father experiences. In eight chapters, Dr. Ken Fuller shares his personal journey of struggling with his own father's absence, the complexities of becoming a father, and the emotional hurdles he faces along the way.

The book delves into themes of identity, love, guilt, redemption, and the fragility of father-child relationships. Ultimately, it emphasizes that fatherhood is not about perfection, but about showing up, learning from mistakes, and offering grace. Through this narrative, the hope is to inspire other fathers to find their voice and answer the question, *Dad, where are you?*

About the Author

Apostle Dr. Ken Fuller, a father of five, believes ministry begins at home, grounding his faith and leadership in family.

After high school, he joined the Marine Corps, learning that "pain is weakness leaving the body." This principle fueled his success in corporate America, where he excelled in management, engineering, and project management, earning certifications like Lean Six Sigma.

At 12, Dr. Ken was called to preach the Gospel. Ordained under the late Rev. Dr. Annie R. Sconier, he completed ministerial studies at New Thought Development Center of Chicago. In 2012, he launched 1 WALK Ministries, which grew into Social Center International Ministries in 2013, a 501(c)(3) serving communities through drives, job fairs, leadership training, and partnerships addressing critical needs like health care and domestic violence. Ministries such as M.A.N. and W3 foster spiritual growth.

Dr. Ken, a pastor to pastors and community activist, travels nationwide spreading the Gospel, mentoring leaders, and teaching through platforms like *Chopping It Up with Apostle Ken* and *The Word Tavern,* which evolved into the School of the Word Institute.

In 2023, he earned an Honorary Doctor of Divinity and Christian Leadership from the School of the Great Commission Bible College.

Today, Dr. Ken pastors, teaches, and leads with grace, rebuilding communities and inspiring growth. Social Center International Ministries remains a place for family, community, and transformation.

Chapter 1: The Missing Piece

You've seen them everywhere. On TV shows like *The Brady Bunch*, *The Cosby Show*, *Family Matters*, and *The Waltons*. They're at baseball games, grocery stores, school plays, and even parent-teacher conferences. These men—the ones called "Dad"—are constant fixtures in the lives of their children. They're there for milestones, pivotal moments, and even the quiet, everyday instances that make a child feel loved and secure.

They give a warm embrace, share a gentle laugh, and hold their children's hands through life's challenges. But what happens when you see them *everywhere else*—except in your life?

What happens when the longing for their presence becomes louder than the absence you've learned to live with? When you come to understand that no matter how strong or independent you grow to be, there's a part of your foundation that's missing?

For me, that realization didn't happen all at once. It wasn't a thunderous moment of clarity but rather a slow, creeping awareness. Like a puzzle piece that didn't quite fit or a shadow that lingered, it was there, unspoken, until I couldn't ignore it anymore.

For those who've read my previous book, *But God: A Journey of Pain, Purpose, and Resilience*, you know that I grew up in a household filled with life. Seven siblings—four boys, three girls—alongside my mother and stepfather. My stepfather, Pops, was a man of great warmth. He wasn't my biological father, but he treated us with love and respect. He worked hard, shared laughs with us, and partnered well with my mother in raising our family.

When he and my mom decided to separate, they did so amicably. Even now, they remain friends. Pops still calls us his sons and daughters, a testament to the bond he built with us. But as much as Pops cared for me, there was always a part of me that wondered about the man whose blood ran through my veins.

Who was my *real* father? Dad where are you? As a child, the absence didn't gnaw at me immediately. Memories from my earliest years—around the age of five or six—are hazy at best. It wasn't until one pivotal moment that the thought of a father, my *father*, began to take root in my mind.

I can still remember the sound. A single, loud gunshot pierced the air, shaking me to my core. I didn't know what it was or why it happened, but it was terrifying. In that moment of fear and confusion, I instinctively yearned for someone to make sense of it all. Someone who could offer me protection and assurance.

It wasn't that my mother wasn't enough—she was an incredible mom who worked tirelessly to provide for us. But there are moments in life when a child longs for the strength of a father, for the steady hand of a man who can shield you from the unknown.

That was the first time I thought, *Dad, where are you?*

At that age, I didn't even know who he was. My mother never spoke ill of him, but she didn't speak of him much at all. I knew I must have a father somewhere—after all, everyone does—but his identity was a mystery to me. It wasn't until we moved from the projects to the South Side of Chicago that the pieces of the puzzle began to come together.

One day, as my mom got me ready for school, she casually mentioned my father. His name was Henry Roberts—Hank, she called him.

Hearing his name for the first time was surreal. It turned him from an abstract idea into a real person. My dad had a name, an identity, a history. He wasn't just a question mark in my life anymore.

My mom told me he was a blue-collar worker, a butcher who owned property and worked hard. She explained that my grandparents on his side were biracial, and somewhere in the intersection of their lives, she and my father had met. I was the result of that meeting.

But her words, as informative as they were, only made my longing grow deeper. I had questions—so many questions.

Was he there when I was born? Did he see my first steps? Did he hear me say "Dada" for the first time? What did he feel when he held me? Did he even hold me at all?

These thoughts swirled in my young mind, but no one could answer them. My memories didn't stretch far enough back to piece it all together, and my mother only shared so much.

Then came the day that changed everything. My mom told me my father was coming to visit. My father.

I was thrilled, nervous, and curious all at once. Who was this man? How tall was he? Was he strong? Rich? Did he look like me? Did I look like him?

The excitement was overwhelming, but so was the confusion. While I anticipated his arrival, questions lingered in my mind: *Dad, where have you been? Dad where are you?*

Despite the questions, I couldn't wait to tell my friends. Back then, having a dad was like having a badge of honor. It gave you a certain kind of confidence, a sense of security. Being able to say "my dad" felt like holding a golden ticket to a world where you were safe, loved, and protected.

Dads were superheroes—protectors, providers, and problem-solvers. To know my dad was coming meant I had my very own superhero.

Looking back, I realize that my longing for my father wasn't just about having someone to call Dad. It was about what he represented—the answers to the questions I didn't even know how to ask.

Why did I feel a void? Why did I look to other families with envy? Why did I feel like something essential was missing from my story?

Even as I prepared for his visit, I knew deep down that one meeting couldn't answer all those questions. But it was a start.

It was my chance to begin a journey toward understanding the man who helped bring me into this world but had been absent from it for so long.

That day, as I waited for him to arrive, I didn't just feel excitement—I felt hope. Hope that the man I had imagined would finally become real. Hope that his presence, even if just for a moment, would fill the gaps in my heart.

But as life would teach me, the journey to understanding my father and my place in his world would be far more complicated than a single visit could resolve.

Still, that day marked the beginning. It was the moment I began to confront the questions, the pain, and the longing that had quietly shaped my childhood. It was the moment I truly began to ask:

Dad, where are you?

Chapter 2: The Day My Father Returned

It was a sweltering summer day in Chicago, and the sun seemed to pour its heat onto the city with relentless intensity. I was dressed in my Sunday best, a mix of nerves and excitement bubbling within me as I prepared to meet my father for the first time—or at least, the first time I could recall. The thought of finally seeing him brought a whirlwind of emotions, anticipation laced with apprehension.

As I stood there waiting, I couldn't help but imagine what the moment would be like. When he arrived, the image of him was etched into my memory instantly. His afro was striking, a dark bronze-black halo around his head. He wore a cream button-up summer shirt paired with tan bell-bottoms and pointed brown shoes that clicked slightly on the pavement as he walked. He looked sharp, confident, and different from anything I had envisioned.

When he saw me, he pulled me in for a hug—a gesture both warm and foreign. I didn't know what to expect, but I felt his effort to connect. He chuckled as he spoke, a peculiar sound that I would later come to associate with him. Instead of calling me Ken, as everyone else did, he affectionately said, "Kenny." It struck me as odd, but I didn't correct him. For the moment, I was simply glad to see him, glad to be acknowledged.

We left together, heading out for a few hours. I didn't say much, being the introverted child that I was. I had always been shy, preferring to stay in my own little world unless I felt truly at ease with someone. Even though this was my father, the situation was new and unfamiliar. I didn't know his likes, his dislikes, or the essence of who he was. To me, he was a blank slate, someone I was just beginning to piece together.

I had envisioned our first meeting differently. Maybe we'd toss a ball in the park, or he'd teach me something cool. But the reality was quite different. What I learned over time was that my dad was a man who took pride in his appearance. I never saw him in sneakers or a tracksuit; he was always sharply dressed, even when casual. That first day, he took me out to eat and introduced me to some of his family members. I met James, a cousin of his who stood out to me because, amusingly, my brother was also named James.

During our time together, my dad often stared at me. It was as if he were in a daze, processing my existence. His gaze felt intense, as though he were grappling with the time lost between us or marveling at how much I resembled him. I didn't fully understand it then, but years later, as I reflected, I realized that he might have been caught in the weight of regret and disbelief.

One moment from that day sticks with me. Cousin James scolded my dad, saying he should have done better by me—bringing me around the family sooner, being more present.

It was a grown-up conversation, so I kept my head down, as my mother had always taught me. "Stay out of grown folks' business," she would say. At the time, I didn't fully process James's words, but they stayed with me, lingering in my subconscious.

That night, I slept soundly for the first time in a while. The excitement of the day filled me with hope. Maybe this was a turning point. I had always dreamed of being able to say the words "my dad" like other kids. Now it seemed that dream was within reach.

Our next meeting came quickly, and I was eager. My dad picked me up, and we made a stop along the way. A woman climbed into the car—a stranger named Sandra. It turned out she was my dad's girlfriend. I was taken aback. It was only our second time together, and I was already sharing him with someone else. I had envisioned these moments as opportunities for us to bond, to get to know each other. Instead, I was navigating the presence of another person in our fragile relationship.

The experience was awkward, especially when they began to argue in front of me. At my age, I didn't have the tools to process what was happening, but I knew it felt wrong. I told my mom about it later, and she confronted my dad—not out of bitterness or jealousy, but as a gentle reminder. She wanted him to understand that his focus should be on building a relationship with me, given how much time we'd already lost.

As an adult, I now see the importance of pacing when introducing children to a new partner. Relationships take time, and children need an even longer period to adjust. Looking back, I felt overwhelmed, trying to understand my dad while also figuring out who this new person was.

Our visits became more frequent, but they followed a predictable pattern. My dad would pick me up, take me to his house, feed me, and then have me do yard work. It was far from what I had hoped for. I had dreamed of us going to the park, taking trips, or simply talking. I wanted him to teach me things—how to throw a football, how to save money, or what it meant to be a man. I wanted guidance, lessons, and the kind of bonding that would prepare me for the world.

But instead, it felt like I was a guest in his life, not a son being embraced fully. He was there physically, but emotionally, there was a distance. I had so many questions: Did my dad love God? Did he believe in Him? Did he attend church? I wanted to know his values, his beliefs, and his thoughts on life. I wanted him to show me how to drive, to teach me how to protect myself, and to explain what it meant to lead a household.

These were the things I longed for, but they seemed just out of reach. I began to understand that presence isn't the same as involvement. A dad can be around without truly being there in the way a child needs.

Looking back now, I see those days through a different lens. As a child, I was hungry for connection, for affirmation, and for guidance. I craved the presence of a father who would not only show up but also pour into me. I've learned that building a relationship takes effort, vulnerability, and intention—qualities that can't be forced but must come from a place of genuine love and commitment.

My father's actions, or lack thereof, taught me valuable lessons about fatherhood. I learned what I didn't want to repeat. I came to understand the importance of showing up fully, not just physically but emotionally and spiritually as well.

For years, I carried the question, *Dad, where are you?* It wasn't about his physical location but about his role in my life. I've come to peace with the complexities of our relationship, but I'll never forget the longing I felt as a child. It shaped me, taught me resilience, and gave me a deeper appreciation for the kind of father I aspire to be.

This chapter of my life was bittersweet, a mix of hope and disappointment. Yet it was also a chapter of growth—a time when I began to realize the importance of being present, being intentional, and being there in the ways that matter most. My journey with my dad wasn't perfect, but it was a part of my story, and for that, I am grateful.

Chapter 3: The Vanishing Hero

The bond between a father and child is often described as sacred, a thread that weaves lessons, love, and identity into the tapestry of a young life. Yet, as I reflect on those days, it feels as though that thread began to fray before it could ever fully strengthen. Something strange and unsettling began to happen during the time I spent with my father—a series of inconsistencies and absences that would carve out a painful chapter in my childhood.

At first, my dad's visits weren't ideal, but they were at least consistent. When he picked me up, our time together wasn't filled with adventures or laughter; it was errands and chores. I didn't understand it then, but even those mundane moments meant something to me. At least he was there. At least I could say I spent time with him, even if it wasn't what I dreamed a father-son relationship would be. However, a shift was coming, one that would leave an indelible mark on my heart.

It started subtly, almost imperceptibly. My dad would tell my mom he was coming to pick me up. My mom, always dutiful, would dress me up and prepare me for his arrival. My excitement would bubble over as I perched on the front porch, my eyes scanning the street for his car. I sat there, hour after hour, imagining all the things we might do together.

But he didn't show up.

"Mom, did you call him?" I would ask, hope clinging to my voice.

"I did, Ken," she'd reply, her tone weary. "He's not answering."

And so, the waiting game began—a cruel pattern of anticipation and disappointment. Sometimes he came, but most times he didn't. When he did come, the visits were brief and hollow. Before I could savor the moments, he would drop me off again, leaving me to grapple with a gnawing emptiness.

Then one day, without warning or explanation, he stopped coming altogether. He didn't call, didn't send a message—nothing. It was as if he had vanished into thin air, leaving a gaping void where his presence had been. I was devastated, angry, and confused. How could he just abandon me like that? What had I done wrong?

I tried to piece together the fragments of my broken heart, but the questions haunted me. Why didn't he come back? Was I not good enough? Did he love me at all? These thoughts swirled in my mind, unchecked, fueling a storm of anger and self-doubt.

To me, having a father was like having a superhero—someone who could protect you, guide you, and make you feel invincible. But my superhero was gone, and I felt powerless in his absence.

In my community, having a father was a badge of honor. Kids with active dads boasted about their weekend adventures, their new bikes, or the games they played together. I had nothing to share. The shame of my father's absence became unbearable, and so I lied.

"We went to the baseball game," I'd say, or, "We saw this awesome movie together." My fabrications painted a picture of a life I wished I had, a bond I desperately craved. But deep down, I was drowning in the truth: my father had abandoned me, and I didn't know why.

The fear of ridicule kept me silent. I knew kids could be cruel, and I didn't want to become the target of their jokes. It was easier to live in a fantasy than face the reality of my father's rejection.

During this time, my dad's cousin James became a familiar presence. James was kind and attentive, often expressing his frustration at my father's absence. He wanted to step in, to fill the gap my father had left behind. But as much as I appreciated James, he wasn't my dad. No one could replace the man I yearned for.

Every boy dreams of having their father by their side. Stepdads, uncles, and mentors can be incredible, but the longing for one's own father is a unique ache. I couldn't help but feel that I was missing something fundamental, a piece of the puzzle that could never be replaced.

The absence of a father leaves scars that run deep. For a boy to grow into a man, he needs a consistent example—a blueprint to follow, a guide to help navigate the challenges of life. Without my father, I had to piece together my understanding of manhood from fragments, observing other men and trying to learn from their actions. Some were good role models; others were not.

Years later, I would see how this gap shaped me. It influenced the way I approached relationships, the way I dealt with conflict, and even the way I saw myself as a father. I promised myself that if I ever had children, I would never abandon them the way my father abandoned me. I knew I wouldn't be perfect, but I was determined to keep my promises, to show up and be present in their lives.

Even as life went on, I couldn't stop thinking about my dad. What was he doing? Did he think about me? Would he ever call and apologize? These questions lived rent-free in my mind, refusing to be evicted. I wanted closure, an explanation—anything to make sense of his disappearance.

I wrestled with feelings of inadequacy, wondering if I had somehow driven him away. Maybe I wasn't good enough, cool enough, or smart enough. These thoughts became a heavy burden, one that I carried into adulthood.

In hindsight, I see how my father's absence taught me some of life's hardest lessons. It taught me about resilience, about picking up the pieces even when it feels impossible. It taught me about the importance of showing up, of keeping promises, and of being there for the people who need you most.

But it also left scars—trauma, unforgiveness, and a lingering sense of regret. These wounds don't heal overnight. They require time,

reflection, and, ultimately, forgiveness. Forgiveness for him, for myself, and for the circumstances that shaped our story.

A father's presence is more than just physical;
it's emotional, mental, and spiritual. It's a guiding light, a source of strength, and a foundation for growth. Without it, boys like me are left
to navigate the world on their own, piecing together their understanding of manhood from
whatever sources they can find.

Even now, as I look back, I see the undeniable
truth: fathers matter. Their love, guidance, and
presence can shape a child's future in pro-
found ways. My story is a testament to what
happens when that presence is missing and
the challenges it creates for a child trying to
make sense of the world.

Though my father's absence shaped me in
ways I'm still uncovering, it also ignited a fire
within me—a determination to be better, to
break the cycle, and to create a different leg-
acy for my own children. His disappearance
may have left a void, but it also taught me the

value of presence, the power of promises kept, and the importance of showing up.

In the end, my story isn't just about loss; it's about growth, resilience, and the enduring hope that one day, the pieces will all make sense.

Chapter 4: The Void of a Father's Presence

In sixth grade, I began to notice something new and exciting—I liked girls. It was an innocent kind of attraction, full of curiosity and awkwardness. The problem was, I had no idea how to talk to them. I didn't know how to ask for a phone number, how to express my feelings, or even how to hold a meaningful conversation. Back then, my peers and I relied on simple notes that read, "If you like me, circle yes or no." That was as sophisticated as it got.

Looking back, I realize how important a father's presence is during moments like these. A father provides guidance, teaching a young boy how to be a gentleman and approach situations with respect and confidence. But I didn't have that.

I remember one incident in sixth grade vividly. There was a girl I liked. We would talk and laugh, and I thought there was a mutual interest. One day, however, she told the teacher I made her feel uncomfortable and accused me of trying to talk to her. In truth, I was trying to talk to her, but I didn't know how. I knew for certain I hadn't said anything inappropriate—my mother wouldn't have tolerated that—but somehow, my actions were misinterpreted.

The teacher took me to the principal's office. The principal spoke to me at length about being careful when interacting with girls and introduced me to a concept I had never heard before: sexual harassment. The conversation overwhelmed me. Tears began to flow, and I couldn't stop crying. I wasn't crying because I had done something wrong—I knew my intentions were pure. I was crying because I felt misunderstood, embarrassed, and alone.

The principal and teacher tried to console me, but it wasn't enough. What I needed in that moment was my father. I needed him to tell me, "It's okay, son. Keep your head up," while also guiding me on how to handle such situations better in the future. That was one of many pivotal moments in my life when I felt the absence of a father most deeply.

Two years later, I graduated eighth grade. I still remember the song our class sang: "There's a Miracle in Store" by Whitney Houston. For me, a miracle would have been having my father there to celebrate that milestone. As I smiled for the pictures, I couldn't help but feel furious inside. I watched other kids' fathers cheering for them, yelling their names across the parking lot. I would have given anything for my dad to be among them. My mom and sister were there, as always, making the day special, but their love couldn't fill the void left by his absence.

During those years, I developed a love for playing softball. We'd play at the park or in the alley, and whenever I had a good game, I wished my dad could have seen it. I wanted him to be proud of me. But he wasn't there.

By 1987, I was preparing for high school, an exciting yet nerve-wracking transition. My older brother, Tony, had been very popular in high school. He played on the football team and had made a name for himself. His reputation helped pave the way for me, but it didn't completely ease my nerves. Freshman year brought challenges—anxiety, gangs, and the pressure to fit in.

I wasn't much of a fighter, but living in the neighborhood, you had to learn how to defend yourself. I often imagined what it would be like if my dad had been there to teach me how to box or stand up for myself, like the dads I saw in movies. Instead, I relied on what we called "hood knowledge" to navigate confrontations.

In my sophomore year, I joined the wrestling team. Wrestling became a significant part of my high school experience. I excelled and developed discipline and confidence. But every time I looked across the gym during a match, I felt that pang of longing. I saw other dads cheering for their sons, offering advice and support, but mine was never there. Friends would occasionally come to support me, but it wasn't the same.

Despite this void, I achieved a lot in high school. I was the president of both the Afro Club and the Drama Club. I was voted "Most Talented," participated in talent shows (winning first place), and was part of the homecoming court. I earned numerous awards and accolades, but my father missed it all—my prom, my graduation, and every accomplishment in between.

I am grateful for the men who stepped into my life to guide and mentor me. They helped fill some of the gaps, but nothing could fully replace the presence of my biological father. His absence left a lingering pain, one I carried into adulthood.

I harbored resentment and unforgiveness toward him for many years. Though I learned to live without him, the scars remained. His absence shaped me in ways I didn't fully understand at the time, creating challenges I had to face as I grew older.

High school was a time of growth and achievement, but it was also a reminder of what I lacked. The accomplishments I earned and the accolades I received should have been moments of shared joy with my father, but instead, they were tinged with sadness. As I reflect on those years, I recognize how deeply the absence of a father can impact a boy's life. It's a wound that heals slowly, if at all, but it also teaches resilience and the importance of showing up for the people you love.

Chapter 5: Finding Myself

High school graduation was supposed to be the start of something new and exciting for me. My initial plan was to enter law enforcement, but life had other ideas. Not long after I graduated, I became a father to my first daughter. To be completely honest, I was just trying to figure life out at that point. I was overwhelmed, uncertain, and searching for direction. Eventually, I made the decision to join the United States Marine Corps. At the time, I didn't fully grasp the significance of that decision, but looking back, it was one of the most pivotal moments of my life.

The truth is, I needed discipline—real discipline, the kind I never received growing up. That type of guidance is typically instilled by a father, but I didn't have one consistently present in my life. My daughter was about two years old when I enlisted, and I joined with a sense of determination. I wanted to become more disciplined, provide a better life for her, and figure out who I was and what I truly wanted in life. At the time, I was impatient, bad with money, and quick-tempered. My mother and grandmother always said, *"Anything easy to come by isn't worth having."* But I struggled to internalize that wisdom.

When you've gone without—whether physically. materially, emotionally, or spiritually—you develop a hunger. It's an aching desire to fill that void immediately. I lived much of my life with that mindset. I wanted everything *now*. And honestly, some remnants of that impatience still linger today. But by God's grace and the conviction of the Holy Spirit, I've learned to tell myself, *"Ken, slow down."* This was the space I found myself in during that time—a young man desperately searching for himself while yearning for the guidance I had missed.

I always hoped for a strong relationship with my father. I imagined he would be the one to lead me, guide me, and help pave the way for me in life. I understood that I had responsibilities too, but having a father's guidance would have made all the difference. Instead, I hit snares, stumbled into rough patches, and struggled to navigate manhood without a consistent role model. My biological father's presence in my life was fleeting—he would appear, only to disappear again. That absence left me feeling abandoned and lost, and it shaped much of the pain and confusion I carried into adulthood.

When I joined the military, I thought it would be the answer to my problems. I believed it would mold me into the man I wanted to become—a man of discipline, strength, and purpose. And to some degree, it did. I learned survival skills, gained structure, and developed a work ethic. But what it didn't fix were the deep emotional wounds I carried.

After my time in the military, life hit me hard. My first love—the mother of my oldest daughter—and I parted ways. That heartbreak left me reeling. Let me be honest: I had no idea how to be a father. None. It's incredibly hard to be something you've never seen modeled for you. Yes, I'd seen other fathers—friends' dads who seemed to have it all together—but I never had a stable, consistent example in my own life. No one ever took me by the hand and said, *"This is how you do it. This is how you take care of your responsibilities as a man."*

I did my best based on what I observed and pieced together from other people's examples. But trying to imitate someone else's parenting style without a foundation of your own is like building a house on sand. It's not sustainable. At that time, I thought being a good dad meant picking my daughter up for the weekend, buying her new shoes, and walking around the mall. But I wasn't instilling in her the morals, values, or spiritual principles that really matter. I didn't talk to her about Jesus. I wasn't planting seeds of faith or teaching her about grace. I was simply doing what I thought fathers were supposed to do—show up, provide, and be stern.

And I was stern. I was no-nonsense. If you ask my oldest daughter, she'll tell you that "Daddy didn't play." I wasn't abusive, but I was rigid. I barely offered grace, and I demanded perfection without considering whether I was giving her the tools to meet those expectations. I was doing the best I could with what I had, but what I had wasn't much.

As I grew older, I began to understand that the best fathers are those who find their identity in God. A father who is connected to God is better equipped to guide, protect, and nurture his children. At that time, I was trying to give my daughter an identity that I had borrowed from others. My approach to fatherhood was a patchwork of things I had seen and admired in other men, but it lacked authenticity because it didn't come from a place of healing or wholeness.

Over time, I realized that being physically present isn't enough. To be a good father, you also need to be physically, emotionally, mentally, and spiritually present. If you're not whole in those areas, it's impossible to give your children the guidance and stability they need.

Looking back, I can admit that much of my time as a father was spent operating from a place of brokenness. I was emotionally unstable and disconnected from God at times, which made it difficult to parent from a place of grace and love.

Fathers, if you're reading this, let me share something important: your presence matters. Not just your physical presence, but your emotional, mental, and spiritual presence, too. Your children need you to be whole so that you can guide them from a place of wisdom and love. There were so many times in my life when I needed someone to tell me, *"Slow down, Ken."* I didn't have that voice, and it led me to make decisions that caused pain and regret.

One of those decisions was developing a gambling addiction after leaving the military. I was searching for something—an escape, a sense of control, or maybe just a way to numb the pain of feeling lost. That addiction cost me dearly. I lost money, time, and opportunities. I fell behind on my rent, my car was repossessed, and I couldn't even afford to provide for my daughter. My best friend quietly stepped in, giving me money for diapers, milk, or even just a slice of pizza for my little girl. I felt small. I felt like a failure. And I started to wonder if my life was even worth living.

It was during one of my darkest moments that God spoke to me. I was at the end of my rope, contemplating suicide, when I heard His voice. He asked me, *"Are you tired?"* And for the first time in a long time, I admitted that I was. In that moment, I felt a glimmer of hope—a small but powerful reminder that my story wasn't over. Yes, I was still broken. Yes, I was still battling emotionally, physically, and spiritually. But I also felt restored, as though God had reached down and reminded me that He wasn't finished with me yet.

I longed to share that experience with my biological father. I wanted him to be part of my healing, to walk alongside me as I tried to rebuild my life. But that wasn't my reality.

Instead, I leaned on God and began to rebuild from the ground up.

As I reflect on those years, I see the importance of planting seeds. Fathers, every word you speak, every lesson you teach, every story you share is a seed. Your children may not understand its value in the moment, but those seeds take root over time. They grow, and one day, they may save your child from making the same mistakes you did.

Life after the military wasn't easy. I faced heartbreak, addiction, financial struggles, and the weight of trying to be a father without a clear blueprint. But through it all, I learned that God can take our brokenness and turn it into something beautiful. I learned that being a father isn't about perfection—it's about presence. It's about showing up, being vulnerable, and allowing God to work through you.

To this day, I continue to grow as a father and as a man. I don't have all the answers, and I still make mistakes. But I've learned to lean on God, to slow down, and to parent from a place of grace and love. My journey hasn't been easy, but it's been worth it. And I pray that my story will inspire others to keep going, to keep growing, and to trust that with God, all things are possible.

Chapter 6: The Fragile Bonds of Fatherhood

Time has a way of moving forward, indifferent to the joy or pain we experience along the way. By the time I found myself in my second marriage, life had grown complicated but rewarding. My wife and I had two children together, bringing my total to five: four daughters and one son. These blessings gave me a sense of purpose, yet they also magnified the absence I had felt since childhood—the void left by my father.

It had been years, perhaps decades, since I had last seen my dad. My memories of him were fleeting, like snapshots of a life interrupted. He was a shadowy figure who appeared sporadically during my teenage years, only to vanish just as quickly. Yet, life has a way of unearthing what you think you've buried for good. Through a family friend, I discovered that my father lived not far from the neighborhood my family had moved to after leaving the projects. He owned property nearby, had a girlfriend, and a son—my younger brother.

Learning this truth stirred something deep within me, a cocktail of emotions that ranged from curiosity to jealousy, and anger to longing. The thought of my father living a life that seemed so complete without me gnawed at my soul. He had started a new family, giving them the time, care, and attention I had always craved. My younger brother had what I never did—a father who was present. It hurt. Badly. But I resolved to push my feelings aside and try to forge a connection with my brother, hoping to salvage something meaningful from the wreckage of my father's absence.

The day I saw my father again, it was as if time had both stood still and sprinted ahead. He was older, his hair streaked with gray, and his body worn by age and illness. He sat in a wheelchair, his health visibly fragile. It was surreal to look at him after so many years.

This man, who should have been a towering figure in my life, now seemed diminished, both physically and emotionally. Yet, he was not alone. My younger brother hovered nearby, their bond apparent in the way they interacted.

I couldn't help but wonder: had my father taught him the things I had desperately wanted to learn? Had he shown him how to be a man, offered him advice, or been there during his toughest moments? Questions raced through my mind, each one a reminder of what I had missed. But I tried to stay focused on the present, grateful for the chance to at least be in his presence again, however bittersweet it felt.

Despite my complicated feelings, I began to build a relationship with my younger brother. He started visiting my home, spending time with me and my family. We laughed together, shared stories, and for a while, it felt like a piece of the puzzle was falling into place. I cherished these moments, even though a part of me resented the circumstances that had made them possible.

His mother, however, didn't seem thrilled about our budding relationship. Her cold demeanor and subtle interference were hard to ignore. Still, I was determined. This was my brother, and I wanted him to know that I was there for him, even if our connection had come late and under less-than-ideal circumstances.

But life has a way of throwing curveballs when you least expect them. Over time, the calls I made to my brother went unanswered. I would stop by his house, knocking on the door, but no one would come to greet me. The silence was deafening, and the rejection—whether intentional or circumstantial—stung deeply. Eventually, I let go, convincing myself that perhaps he needed space or that his mother's influence had driven a wedge between us.

Years passed, and my relationship with my brother became a memory I tried not to dwell on. Then, one day, a persistent feeling led me to drive by his house. I spotted the family friend who had first told me where my father lived. After a brief conversation, he dropped a bombshell: my father had passed away.

The news hit me like a freight train. I felt a wave of emotions crash over me—grief, regret, anger, and an overwhelming sense of loss. I thought of the time we had wasted, the questions I never asked, and the answers I would never receive. Tears streamed down my face as I became challenged with the reality that my father was gone.

I remembered visiting him in a nursing home during his final days. His smile, faint but genuine, had touched something deep within me. Yet, that memory now felt hollow.

 I didn't want to remember him as a frail man in a wheelchair; I wanted to recall moments of joy, connection, and the father-son bond we had never truly built. But life is rarely so kind. Sometimes, all you have are fragments of what could have been.

As I processed the loss of my father, I decided to check on my brother. The family friend knocked on his door, and after a moment, my brother emerged. He looked different—his face drawn, his energy subdued. When I asked how he was doing, he revealed something that made my heart sink: he had been battling cancer.

Hearing this was like a punch to the gut. My brother, my connection to my father, was facing his own mortality. I felt helpless, unsure of how to support him through such a harrowing experience. My wife and I offered our help, but he seemed determined to face this battle alone.

Despite his isolation, he eventually emerged victorious, surviving cancer and proving his resilience. Yet, our relationship remained distant, leaving me with more questions than answers.

As time went on, I found myself growing angrier with my father. His death felt like a betrayal, a final abandonment that robbed me of the chance to mend our fractured relationship. I couldn't shake the thought: *He left before he could make things right.*

I had always imagined a reunion where we would reconcile, where the pain of the past would dissolve into a newfound closeness. But that dream had died with him, leaving me to navigate a sea of unresolved emotions. I was angry at the years we had lost, the lessons he hadn't taught me, and the love he hadn't given. But as much as I wanted to cling to my anger, I knew it wouldn't serve me. Life is too short to dwell on what could have been.

In the wake of my father's death, I faced a decision: I could let the pain consume me, or I could choose to heal. I chose the latter, though it wasn't easy. I began to focus on the family I had built, pouring my energy into being the father I had always wanted for myself.

My children would not grow up wondering if they were loved or valued. They would know, every single day, that they mattered.

I also tried to let go of the bitterness I felt toward my father. I realized that while our relationship was far from perfect, it had shaped me in ways I hadn't fully understood. His absence taught me the importance of presence. His shortcomings as a father motivated me to be better. And while I still wished things had been different, I knew that holding onto regret would only hold me back.

The fragile bonds of fatherhood are often tested by time, circumstance, and human imperfection. My story is not unique; it's a reflection of the complex relationships many of us have with our parents. But it's also a reminder that even in the face of loss and disappointment, there is room for growth, forgiveness, and love.

As I look back on my journey, I see not just the pain but also the lessons it taught me. I see the strength it gave me to overcome, the wisdom to value what truly matters, and the courage to keep moving forward.

My father may not have been the man I needed him to be, but his absence pushed me to become the man I was meant to be. And for that, I am grateful.

This is my truth, and it's a truth I will carry with me as I continue to navigate the complexities of life, love, and family.

Chapter 7: The Unseen Struggle: A Father's Journey Through Love, Guilt, and Redemption

Being a father is one of the most rewarding yet challenging roles a man can undertake. For those who are married or in a stable relationship, with their children living under the same roof, fatherhood might seem more accessible.

But even in these seemingly ideal circumstances, complexities arise. My own journey as a father has been far from perfect, marked by a sense of division, guilt, and redemption—a reflection of both my triumphs and shortcomings.

When my father passed away, I was still married to my second wife. Together with our two youngest daughters, we lived in the same household. Meanwhile, my three older chil-dren—my son and two eldest daughters—would visit periodically. Yet, despite these visits, I felt a strain in my relationships with them.

A part of me attributed this disconnect to the dynamics of my new family arrangement, where I was fully present with two of my children while the others lived apart. It was a painful echo of my own childhood, where my father's choice to start a new family left me feeling overlooked and distant.

For a long time, guilt consumed me. I wrestled with the idea that I was repeating the same pattern I had resented in my father. But as time went on, I realized that I also deserved to build a life and create stability for my family.

 Life does go on, and while my father's absence shaped me, it didn't define my capacity to love my children. I was determined to be the kind of father who showed up—physically, emotionally, and financially. If I promised my children something, I delivered, even if it meant personal sacrifice. Many times, I went without things I needed, a fact their mothers were often unaware of. Yet, no matter how much I gave, the guilt lingered.

I had always envisioned the ideal family: two parents raising their children together in harmony, attending games, performances, and church services, and celebrating milestones as a unit.

This vision was far from my reality, and the gap between what I dreamed and what I lived weighed heavily on me. My children—especially those who lived outside my home—undoubtedly felt the distance. I imagine they often wondered, *Dad, where are you?*

Balancing my roles as a husband and a father, all while grappling with my own unresolved issues from my father's absence, felt like an insurmountable task. I often compared myself to friends who seemed to navigate fatherhood effortlessly. Their connections with their children appeared seamless, while I struggled to maintain mine.

The disagreements with my older children's mothers added another layer of difficulty. At times, conflicts between us became obstacles to seeing my children, although I know their mothers meant well. We were all young, maturing, and trying to figure out life.

Looking back, I wish I'd had my father's guidance to navigate these challenges. But I did the best I could with the knowledge and maturity I had at the time. There were moments when I simply shut down, avoiding arguments to keep the peace. This avoidance, however, came at a cost.

The term *baby mama drama* is often thrown around lightly, but it's a real phenomenon that can cause estrangement and deep emotional scars. I've learned that when parents allow their conflicts to overshadow their shared responsibility, it's the children who suffer most.

To every parent, whether single, engaged, or married, I offer this advice: Ask God for guidance. Pray for the maturity to prioritize your children above personal grievances. Children should never be caught in the crossfire of adult conflicts. The goal should always be to create a stable and loving environment, no matter the circumstances.

I'll admit, I wasn't a perfect father. I made mistakes—some small, others significant. Yet, my love for my children never wavered. I wanted to love them better than my father loved me. I longed to give them the kind of affection and attention I had yearned for. While we shared countless joyful moments filled with laughter, pranks, and silly songs, there were also struggles. Time and again, I found myself grappling with how to be present for all of them equally.

As my children grew older, the challenges evolved. They began making their own choices—some of which mirrored mistakes I had made. Watching them stumble was agonizing because I recognized the paths they were heading down. My response was often harsh, driven by my desire to protect them from pain. In hindsight, I realize my approach sometimes pushed them further away.

The balance between offering guidance and maintaining a strong bond is delicate, and I didn't always get it right.

My relationship with my eldest daughter is a poignant example. We were incredibly close when she was younger, but as she grew and made her own decisions, our connection became strained. It wasn't a lack of love; it was life taking its course.

I struggled to reconcile my role as a father who wanted to shield her from harm with her need to live her life on her terms. Despite the distance, I am immensely proud of the woman and mother she has become. I pray for her daily, trusting that our bond, though altered, remains strong.

Out of my five children, I poured a particular intensity into my relationship with my son. Not out of favoritism, but because I saw in him a reflection of myself—a boy who would one day become a man. I wanted to equip him with the tools I had lacked. We talked about everything: finances, relationships, hard work, and even vulnerability.

We laughed, cried, and faced life's challenges together. Yet, even with the time and effort I invested, I sometimes questioned whether I had done enough.

Fatherhood is a paradox. It is as fulfilling as it is demanding. Shows like *The Cosby Show* or *Family Matters* make it look simple, but real life is far more complex. I now have five children—four daughters and one son—

and I still find myself navigating the challenges of being a father without having had one as a guide. Yet, I refuse to dwell on my shortcomings. Instead, I take responsibility for my mistakes and commit to doing better.

To the fathers out there, know this: We are not defined by our failures. We can choose to repair broken relationships and build stronger connections, one step at a time. Regardless of how strained or distant things may seem, we are always fathers to our children. Our role is lifelong, and so is our opportunity to make a positive impact.

Yes, fatherhood can be a thankless job. There are times when we feel overlooked, taken for granted, or only contacted when financial needs arise. But our purpose as fathers goes beyond recognition. We are called to provide, protect, and guide, just as God does for us. When the weight of this responsibility feels overwhelming, I find comfort in Proverbs 3: Trust in the Lord with all your heart, lean not on your own understanding, and He will direct your path.

I no longer blame myself for my past mistakes. Instead, I focus on what I can do today to be the best father I can be. To every man facing similar struggles, I urge you to stand up, seek God's wisdom, and work diligently to rebuild and strengthen your relationships with your children. Fatherhood is not easy, but it is a divine calling. Let us embrace it with humility, perseverance, and love.

Chapter 8: Fatherhood: A Journey of Imperfection and Grace

For a long time, I've felt a deep need to share my journey through fatherhood. To every father out there, I want to begin by saying this: we may never fully "get it right." There isn't a perfect formula for fatherhood. You'll often hear people say, "I have the perfect father," or "I have the perfect mother." But if you were to hear those parents' honest stories, they'd probably tell you they fall far short of perfection. True love for your children pushes you to hold yourself to a high standard—a standard that, at times, feels impossible to meet.

If I could offer one piece of advice to fathers, fathers-to-be, and those who aspire to fatherhood someday, it would be this: do not take on the responsibility of being a father without first surrendering your life to Jesus Christ.

When you have a relationship with God, He becomes your guide, comforter, and teacher. He helps you navigate moments of high emotions, teaching you not just what to say but how to say it. Fatherhood doesn't come with a manual, but walking with God provides the ultimate blueprint.

Many men, myself included, enter fatherhood carrying the weight of unresolved trauma. For those who grew up without a father or without a consistent father figure, there's often a battle within—how can you be what you've never seen? This pain, this absence, can manifest in pride and denial, leaving wounds unhealed. But I urge you, don't bury those emotions. Ask God for the courage to face them, to release them, and to begin the journey of healing. Only then can you pour love and support into your children from a whole and healthy place.

Too often, fathers who lacked the presence of their own dads attempt to parent from a broken place. But the reality is, this is not a time to remain broken. Your children face battles in a world that is constantly changing and challenging them. They need you whole. To achieve this, you must dig deep and find a way to forgive.

Forgive your father for his absence or shortcomings, no matter how painful it may be. In doing so, you free yourself to be the man and father God has called you to be.

Even with faith as our foundation, mistakes are inevitable. None of us will ever achieve perfect fatherhood, and that's okay. If God expected perfection from us, there would've been no need for Jesus. The goal isn't to strive toward imperfection, but rather to strive toward growth and excellence.

Just as we must forgive our fathers, we must also forgive ourselves. Right now, as you read this, there are men wrestling with guilt—sitting in cars, at desks, in the gym or on long drives—haunted by feelings of inadequacy. They believe they've failed as fathers or lack the tools to succeed.

Some of these men seem strong on the outside. They hold prestigious titles, manage businesses, or even lead nations. But behind closed doors, they cry silently, burdened by the belief that they are falling short in the lives of their children. It's a constant battle, one that requires accountability, humility, and perseverance. Becoming the father you aspire to be might take weeks, months, or even years, but the key is to never stop trying.

If all you can give your children is one dollar, give it. And above all, be consistent. Keep your promises. If you say you're going to show up, do so. While you may not make it to every game, recital, or school event, the moments you are there matter deeply.

To your children, you are their superhero. They see you as invincible, even when you're struggling inside. Strive to live up to their perception—not by being flawless, but by being present and leading with love.

Fatherhood requires balance. Discipline with a stern hand when necessary, but always lead with grace and understanding. Our children will make mistakes, just as we did. Meet them where they are, listening without judgment, and guide them with wisdom. Encourage them to share their perspectives, dreams, and fears. These moments of connection build trust and nurture a relationship that will withstand life's challenges.

It's also critical to consider the foundation you're building before becoming a father. Know the woman you choose to parent with. Take time to see her character in all seasons. Is she someone who will walk in wisdom and protect your role as a father, even if the relationship doesn't work out?

A supportive partner will never weaponize your shortcomings against you or your ability to parent. She will understand that while financial responsibility is essential, fatherhood is far more than monetary contributions.

Society has distorted the concept of child support. Money is important, yes—it keeps the lights on, puts food on the table, and covers necessities. But true child support is about presence, consistency, and love. It's about showing up, not just in person, but emotionally and spiritually. It's about being the father who listens, encourages, apologizes when necessary, and always reinforces your love for your children. Even when they make choices you don't agree with, stand ready to receive them with open arms.

Sometimes, despite our best efforts, the world wins over the foundation we've laid. This isn't always a reflection of poor parenting. Consider the parable of the prodigal son. His father provided for him, but when the son believed he was ready for independence, the father released him. The son's journey was filled with hardship, but when he returned, the father welcomed him back with grace and love. As fathers, we must be willing to do the same.

As you build your life, remember that your children are always watching. If you enter a new relationship, approach it with caution and patience. Your children deserve the stability of seeing their father make thoughtful, deliberate choices. Avoid rushing new partners into their lives. Instead, let your actions show that their well-being is your priority. When handled with care, your children will respect and appreciate the balance you maintain between your life and theirs.

There have been countless moments in my life when I've asked, "Dad, where are you?" In those moments of weight and pressure, I've had to face the same question from my children, whether spoken or unspoken. Their eyes look to me for guidance, integrity, and love. To provide that, I must strive to be the example I want them to follow. If I want them to grow into individuals of character, honesty, and service, I must model those values in my own life.

To every father reading this: you are courageous. You are strong. You are mighty. You are everything God has called you to be. No matter how complex your situation may be, as long as you have breath in your body, you still have time. Fatherhood is a journey, not a destination. Keep striving, keep growing, and be the best father you can be. I love you!